**DISCARDED**

Y0-BLS-803

COPY 1

AYR BRANCH

J 340 .112 Law

Law, Cheryl.
Justice / Cheryl Law and Kaye Stearman. -- Hove, England : Wayland, 1993.
48 p. : ill. (some col.) ; 25 cm. -- (Human rights)

Includes bibliographical references (p. 45-46) and index.
06918654   ISBN:0750206446

1. Justice.   I. Stearman, Kaye.   II. Title

37    93OCT25           07/    1-00613159

# Human Rights

# JUSTICE

Cheryl Law and
Kaye Stearman

Wayland

**Titles in the Human Rights series**

Clean Environment
Food
Freedom of Expression
Homeland
Justice
Shelter

**Acknowledgements**
The authors would like to thank the following individuals and organizations for their help and support: Paul Crook, Richard Dunstan, Leah Levin, Yvonne Terlingen, Rachel Warner, Amnesty International, UNICEF.

Cover illustrations: *background* Student demonstration in Beijing, China in May 1989; *inset* Chengdu detention centre, China

First published in 1993 by
Wayland (Publishers) Ltd
61 Western Road, Hove
East Sussex BN3 1JD
England

© Copyright 1993 Wayland (Publishers) Ltd

Editor: Cath Senker
Designer: Joyce Chester

**British Cataloguing in Publication Data**
Law, Cheryl
Justice. – (Human Rights)
I. Title II. Stearman, Kaye
340.112

ISBN 0-7502-0644-6

Typeset by Dorchester Typesetting Group Ltd, England
Printed and bound by G. Canale C.S.p.A, Turin, Italy

**Picture acknowledgments**
The authors and publishers would like to thank the following for allowing illustrations to be reproduced in this book: Amnesty International 8, 27, (H Zehr) 28, 36, 39; Chapel Studios (Z Mukhida) 35; Eye Ubiquitous 40; Format (B Prince) 6, (J Matthews) 22, (J O'Brien) 24; Frank Spooner Pictures (J Chiasson) 29; Impact (M Ansar) 18; Kobal Collection 5, 32; Notre Dame High School (M Clarke) 38; Panos (A Legarsmeur) *cover* (inset), (T Page) 12, (A Legarsmeur) 13, (B Tobiasson) 15, (H Davies) 23, (S Sprague) 37; Photri 10, (M DiRosa) 14; Popperfoto 20, (Gonzalez) 42; Rex Features 11; Paul Smith 31; Topham *cover* (background), (Daemmrich) 25, 33; United Nations 9, 43; Wayland (Z Mukhida) 41; Zefa (Dr Baer) 19, 21.

# Contents

1 What is the 'right to justice'?
*page 4*

2 Justice and the legal system
*page 10*

3 Poor people and justice
*page 15*

4 Access to justice
*page 19*

5 Punishment and the death penalty
*page 24*

6 Justice denied by the State: 'disappearances' and illegal killings
*page 30*

7 Justice in our lives
*page 35*

Glossary
*page 44*

Further reading
*page 45*

Useful addresses
*page 47*

Index
*page 48*

It should be emphasized that although the material in this book is derived from the experiences of real people in real situations, the characters themselves are fictitious (with the exception of Dalton Prejean) and should not therefore be seen to be representing the experiences of particular persons.

# 1

# What is the 'right to justice'?

'I MEAN, it's not fair, is it? The teacher's always picking on me and Lisa. She is, honest. We're just sitting there and she says we've been talking, when we haven't. She sent me to the Deputy Head, who wouldn't listen either, she banned me from the lunchtime disco. Grown-ups! They never give you a chance to explain. They always do the talking. My mum's the same. It's just not fair.'

(Debbie, 13)

What Debbie has to say about adults is a common complaint in schools and homes everywhere. Young people might think that the way some adults treat young people is a fact of life. But what Debbie is complaining about is the key to answering some basic questions about the right to justice.

Although considering the right to justice can seem very complicated, the idea of fairness is something we all understand from a very early age. 'It's not fair' is a frequent cry from young children. It might be about more space in the playground for the girls when the boys are playing football there; being sent to bed early and missing a television programme; an older brother or sister having more pocket money. Whatever the circumstances, 'it's not fair' is all about how we, when we are younger, see our entitlement, or right, to fair treatment in the world.

As we get older, the cry changes to 'I demand justice', but the meaning and ideas behind it are very much the same. So where does this idea of justice come from and why should we all have this right?

The moral sense of what is fair or unfair, this right to justice, seems to be an in-built feeling that we have. That is why it is said to come from an idea called natural justice. Natural justice is what we are all entitled to as people; it is something we can all claim, that no one else has a right to take away from us, and which we all owe one another. As Eleanor Roosevelt, an American diplomat and humanitarian of the mid-twentieth century, said: 'Justice cannot be for one side alone, but must be for both . . .' Natural justice gives us a sense of when behaviour is unjust, or, more simply, unfair.

*This photograph from a scene in a modern film*, Robin Hood, Prince of Thieves, *shows Robin Hood and his supporters in the forest.*

The legend of Robin Hood is often used in Britain as an example of natural justice and most countries have a similar champion of the people. But how would we solve the moral problem of deciding whether Robin Hood's behaviour was just?

In the story, the rich landlords got their wealth from the serfs living on their land. In return for being allowed to live there, serfs had to give the landlord part of their crops and they had to work on his land as well. The serfs were left in terrible poverty. The landlords often used violence to take the crops. Robin Hood and his supporters saw this as an injustice. They stole money from the landlords and returned it to the serfs.

How can we measure whose behaviour was just and fair? The landlords in the story were acting according to the law; Robin Hood was acting according to natural justice, or fairness.

5

*The idea of fairness can start with very simple things, like the size of your school lunch.*

Justice in society takes two forms. One applies to everyone in society and is about treating everyone equally as a group. This is also called social justice. A simple example can be found in the school canteen. If a canteen worker is serving the food, everyone expects that he or she will give the same portion of food to each pupil – that would be fair. Similarly, if it is a self-service canteen, we should only help ourselves to a fair amount of food, so that there is enough for other people. In that way we are showing responsibility towards other people who have the same rights as ourselves.

Then there is the kind of justice applied to the individual, which comes close to giving each person what they deserve. This is usually when someone is to be punished and the punishment must be of the same level as the wrong that the person has done, if it is to be just. Going back to Debbie; she might well have been talking when she had been told not to, but was being banned from the lunchtime disco a fair punishment?

Social justice means that everyone should be treated the same. This equality is our right as human beings; it is independent of race, gender, religion, political beliefs, sexual orientation or disability. Such justice applies to legal, social and economic standards. The word 'justice' is often immediately connected with the law, but that is only one aspect of the right to justice, which will be considered in the next chapter. Social and economic justice are other strands of the right to justice.

Equal access to education, housing, employment and health care is what we mean by social justice. But the most basic right is economic justice. Economic justice ensures freedom from poverty. If you are poor, you will find it difficult to obtain a good education and adequate housing. You will find it even harder to get legal justice. There will be many examples of how this happens in the chapters that follow.

The right to legal, social and economic justice is protected in a country's written constitution. Most countries in the world have a constitution that incorporates human rights. Ideally, this constitution should protect the rights of all its citizens, including their right to justice. In countries where there is democracy, people can vote against a government that is not maintaining their rights. But many governments that are not democratic publicly declare support for the constitution, although in fact they abuse the human rights included in it.

Many schools in Canada have Student Councils that give pupils an opportunity to participate in the running of some aspects of school life. Pupils from each year group are elected by their fellow pupils to act as their representatives on the Council. They put forward their year group's ideas and suggestions, and in some schools they can also take pupils' complaints to the Council. Pupils who take part in running their school are gaining valuable knowledge about how a democratic government operates, and how each section of society makes its claims for fair treatment.

*Harriet Tubman (c.1820–1913), a slave who worked to abolish slavery in America.*

The idea of citizenship, where natural justice and democracy apply to everyone, is relatively modern. There have been popular movements throughout history in which people worked together to achieve justice. But often, even when they succeeded, there were people who were still left out, and they had to continue with their struggle for justice. The English Magna Carta (1215) is often said to be the basis of Britain's unwritten constitution. It stated that 'to no one will we sell, deny or delay right or justice', but it only applied to 'freemen'. People who were serfs working for a landlord were not included. The American Declaration of Independence (1776) and the US Bill of Rights (1791) left thousands of black men, women and children in slavery. The French Declaration of the Rights of Man and of the Citizen (1789) did not apply, in practice, to women.

This book demonstrates that standards of justice around the world vary according to political systems, and to how justice is protected and enforced. However, a people's right to fair treatment does not only depend on the individual country's constitution or laws. There are also international laws which can be used to defend the right to justice world-wide.

In 1945, after the horror of the Second World War, Britain, the USA, China, the USSR and France invited forty-six other countries to join with them in forming the United Nations. They signed the United Nations Charter, which aimed to promote peace and human welfare. In 1948, the Universal Declaration of Human Rights (see p. 43) set out the rights to which everyone is entitled. Governments which have signed this Declaration promise to uphold these rights in their own country. There are international

*This picture by Japanese children shows Article 2 of the Universal Declaration of Human Rights, which says that everyone should have all the rights in the Declaration no matter what their race, colour, sex or religion.*

*The headquarters of the United Nations in New York, USA, where the General Assembly of the UN meets with representatives from all around the world, to try to find peaceful solutions to the conflicts that exist between the member states.*

courts and procedures which can be used by the citizens of those countries, should the government abuse their human rights. The rights to legal, social and economic justice are included in this Declaration.

Since 1948 there have been many more international laws passed in an attempt to protect people's rights, and in 1990 the Convention on the Rights of the Child came into power. Millions of children and young people around the world under the age of eighteen are unable to exercise their rights to legal, social and economic justice. Some 100 million children live on the streets with no access to even basic education; approximately 155 million children under five live in total poverty and about 12.9 million were expected to die in 1992 from common illnesses and malnutrition. The Convention sets the standards for all governments to protect children from harm and allow them to grow into healthy adults.

At the start of this chapter, our friends, Debbie and Lisa, felt that some of their rights to fair treatment were not being respected by their teachers and parents. And as we also saw, the rights of different groups can conflict – of brothers and sisters, of pupils in the playground, of adults and young people. We can only sort out those problems if we all understand that every right carries with it a responsibility. The biggest responsibility is to respect everyone's rights and by protecting other people's rights, we also protect our own.

# 2

# Justice and the legal system

THE idea of providing fairness for all has evolved into protection by a legal system. A legal system is an elaborate system of rules that lays down how individuals should behave towards one another, how governments should behave towards individuals and how individuals can join together in organizations (such as companies or trade unions).

The basic law that lays down how a country is to be governed is constitutional law, which should also aim to protect our basic human rights. The biggest part of the legal system deals with civil or commercial law (such as company law, trade union law, taxation). The part of the law dealing with most serious crimes by individuals is called criminal law.

In criminal law basic rules should be followed. One of these is that a person is innocent until proven guilty. Another is that everyone has the right to

*A typical modern courtroom in Florida, USA. The judge sits at the raised bench (desk) at the front of the room. The two lawyers, the prosecutor and the defender, stand before the judge to argue their cases.*

*Chairman Mao Zedong, who helped to found the Chinese Communist Party and led it to power in 1949.*

be heard and to be represented by a lawyer of their choice. Witnesses should be cross-examined (questioned) by both sides, in an attempt to find out the truth. Trials should not be secret. The judge and jury should be neutral and unbiased.

While the scope of criminal law varies from country to country, it normally includes crimes against property (such as robbery or vandalism) and crimes against the person (such as assault, rape or murder). The purpose of criminal law should be to protect society from wrong-doers, but in many countries criminal law is misused against people who do not agree with the policies of the government.

One country where this has happened is China. For centuries, China had very strict laws and people could be severely punished for small offences. When the Communist Party came to power in 1949, some of its leaders said that there should be no strict laws and no legal system. Instead the government would decide the rules, which could be changed according to circumstances. This was supposed to be a better way to judge people.

But in practice this system gave government officials a great deal of power. Some became corrupt or brutal but few were punished for it. However, people who disagreed with the government could easily be punished since they had no protection under the law. More and more Chinese people became dissatisfied with this system. They wanted laws that stopped corrupt officials from doing anything they liked, and they demanded that basic human rights be protected by the law.

*In April 1989 hundreds of university students began a hunger strike in Tiananmen Square, central Beijing. They wanted the Chinese Government to introduce democratic reforms. Many thousands joined the protests.*

One person who protested was Li Li, a law student at a university in central China. Li Li isn't her real name; she told her story secretly to a foreign journalist and fears that if she is identified she will be arrested again. But she wanted people outside China to understand what is happening there. This is her story:

'I was born in Shanghai in 1970. My parents had been teachers but in 1965 the government suddenly closed down all the schools and they were sent hundreds of kilometres away to work in the fields with the peasants. Years later they were able to move to Xian and take up teaching again. They were pleased when I got a university place to study law but they warned me to be careful.

'At first I just concentrated on my studies. But I began to realize that the law I was studying was nearly all about rules and regulations and not about people's rights and responsibilities. At another time, I might not have questioned this, but, at the beginning of 1989, the university students were full of new ideas about democracy and human rights. It was very exciting.

'For hours my friends and I discussed these new ideas. We formed a small magazine called *Ming Tian* [Tomorrow]. Actually it was only two pages long and there was never enough paper to print all the copies we needed, so we pasted copies on walls for people to read. One article I wrote was called 'Laws to protect people, not the Communist Party'. It said that since China had signed the UN Universal Declaration of Human Rights we should respect its standards. We heard that in the capital, Beijing, students were occupying Tiananmen Square and refusing to leave until changes were made in the government. We demonstrated to support their demands.

'Then, suddenly, it all ended. On 4 June 1989 the army came into the university and began shooting at us. Some of us fell, killed or wounded. I escaped and hid with friends. But I was soon found by the security forces, beaten and sent to a detention centre outside the city. Foreigners think that it only happened in Beijing, but it was everywhere.

*Prisoners in a detention centre in Chengdu, western China. Facilities are poor and the prisoners must work hard. Conditions in the labour camps, where political prisoners are sent, are even worse.*

'Being a law student, I knew what the law said should happen. Chinese law says that the longest time a person should be detained between arrest and trial should be five and a half months. I was held for over eight months. I was kept alone in a small cell. Every few days I would be taken from my cell and told to confess my crimes. When I said I had nothing to confess, the officer said: "I am the law; I do as I like". When I didn't confess, I was beaten and once I was given electric shocks. I had no visitors and I worried all the time about my parents.

*Huge demonstrations in support of the students in Tiananmen Square took place in many cities around the world. Here, Chinese students are protesting in New York, USA.*

'I didn't have a fair trial. I was charged with "counter-revolutionary acts", but there were no real charges. I didn't choose my lawyer, and in any case, I only saw him a few days before the trial. I wanted to plead "not guilty" but the lawyer said that I wasn't allowed to. Then I said that I would defend myself, but that wasn't allowed either. The witnesses for the prosecution just stood there and lied. There was no chance to cross-examine them. Everyone knew that the verdict would be "guilty", even before the trial started. I was sentenced to four years in a labour camp.

'The other prisoners were common criminals and the prison guards asked them to beat me and the other political prisoners. But actually the criminals were far more humane than the guards. In the winter they shared their clothes and blankets with me. We had to work all day, every day. The food was dreadful, sometimes just a bit of potato or watery soup. I caught tuberculosis but there was no medical help.

'I was released in late 1991 after almost two years there. I don't know why they let me go early. Of course, I couldn't return to university and I'm not allowed to work. The police spy on me and it's difficult to talk freely to anyone. I still suffer from the effects of my years in prison. But I won't give up my ideas.'

# 3

# Poor people and justice

IN most countries all people have, in theory, equal rights before the law. However, this does not mean that justice is equally available to all people. For example, richer people are more likely to be able to afford a lawyer who can present their case in court, while poorer people may have to go without a lawyer. Courts and lawyers are usually based in towns and cities, far from people who live in villages or in remote rural areas. Court cases may continue for weeks or months – or even years.

People who know their legal rights are more likely to receive justice before the law than those who do not. In some countries, such as India, many people are illiterate and cannot read the relevant legal documents, like an arrest warrant or a court order.

*A village in Bihar, northern India. In Bihar there are a few landlords who own thousands of acres, but most farmers possess only an acre or two each.*

They might put their thumb-print on these documents, without understanding their contents. Perhaps they speak a language different from the one used in the courts, and therefore they can't follow what is happening.

Sometimes whole groups of people have low status in society. Perhaps they or their ancestors were servants or slaves and were expected always to obey their masters and mistresses. If they didn't, they were often beaten. This is the case in India, where a system of social groups called castes developed. The lowest castes were known as 'untouchables'.

When people are regarded as inferiors rather than as equals, it is almost impossible for them to obtain justice. Clearly they also need other rights, known as social and economic rights, to be recognized. These include the right to adequate food, clothing and housing, to employment at fair wages, education, good health and the right to be treated equally with other people. All these rights, together with others, are expressed in international human rights standards. As we saw in Chapter 1, social and economic rights are the foundation for all of our other human rights.

India is one country which has made social and economic rights a part of its law. The Indian constitution of 1950 states that all citizens should have 'justice – social, economic and political' and 'equality of status and opportunity'. The 'untouchables', renamed the Scheduled Castes, were given special protection and extra help in education and employment. But in many areas life has hardly changed for most 'untouchables'. Today some 'untouchables' call themselves *dalits* – the oppressed ones.

Buddu was only twelve years old when he was arrested and beaten by the police in his home town of Sonari in Bihar, north India. Buddu's family are very poor, like most of the people in Bihar. They also belong to an 'untouchable' caste.

Buddu's father, Suresh Musahar, came from a small village in central Bihar. Because he owned no land, he worked for the local landlord. The wages were so low that the family could barely manage one poor meal a day. But when Suresh asked for higher wages, he was beaten by the landlord. That night, fearing further beatings, the family fled the village. Eventually, they settled in Sonari, where Suresh found work and Buddu attended school.

Buddu tells his story: 'Early one morning several policemen arrived. They said that they wanted to arrest my friend Nakul Bagti but they didn't say why. When his family tried to protest, they were beaten. Then the police said that there had been a robbery and the robbers were from our *basti* [neighbourhood]. They seized Nakul and Shankar Ram and myself, and threw us in the police van, beating us all the time. I was so frightened that I couldn't stop crying.

'At the *thana* [police station] they beat us with *lathis* [sticks] and soon we were covered with bruises. We felt as though all our bones were breaking inside us. We were thrown into a small cell. Sometimes they would pull one of us out, beat him, stop for a while and start again. The beatings went on for two days and two nights.'

Indian law says that when people are arrested they must be brought before a magistrate (judge) within twenty-four

*In India it is common for children to be treated brutally by the police, especially poor and low-caste children, who often live and work on the city streets.*

hours and then either released on bail or sent to jail to await trial. But the three boys remained at the police station for three days before this happened. The police produced records before the court saying that the boys had been arrested only the day before, just as they were about to commit a robbery.

Buddu continues: 'When we went into court we were covered in bruises and Nakul started vomiting blood, but no one asked why. It was very confusing. I suppose I was lucky because the magistrate let me go. I thought at first he might have felt sorry for me because I was so small and I was crying, but later I learnt that my father had got some money together and paid the police to say that it was all a mistake and that I wasn't involved. But Nakul and Shankar were sent to Sakchi jail. We heard that Nakul died in hospital the next day. There were marks all over his body.'

There was so much anger in Sonari about the death of Nakul in police custody that the people from the *basti* decided to protest. They marched through the town, chanting 'we want justice' and 'punish the police'. When they reached the government offices, they sat down in the road and refused to move until the district magistrate and the chief of police promised to investigate Nakul's death.

Buddu's father, Suresh, joined the protest. He explained: 'The police come often to the *basti* and we know that they will beat us if we don't pay them something. When the police took Buddu I feared the worst. So I went to my employer and begged him to lend me money so I could get Buddu away from the police. If we all join together to protest maybe we can get something done.'

The Bihar government said that any police officer who was found guilty of beating the boys would be punished.

*This sign outside a Hindu holy place in India says that there should be no discrimination against people because of their caste.*

The police officer in charge of Sonari *thana* was temporarily suspended from his post. But in the end none of the policemen were punished. The Bihar government gave Nakul Bagti's family some money as compensation for his death. The family felt cheated of justice but they needed the money.

For Buddu and Shankar the memories remain of the beatings and they fear that one day the police will return for them. Suresh too is worried. 'We left the village to escape the violence of the landlord. Will we have to leave Sonari to escape the violence of the police? They wouldn't beat us if we were rich or high caste. Will people like us ever be treated properly?'

# 4

# Access to justice

LEGAL systems aim to give everyone an equal chance of receiving justice through the law. There are a few cases where there are good reasons for differences in the law for different groups of people. Some groups are already in a disadvantaged position and so should have special protection. For example, because children are still developing their minds and bodies, it would be unfair to expect them to undertake all the legal rights and responsibilities of adults.

This doesn't mean that children shouldn't have human rights. Very young children need their rights to be protected by adults, such as parents, guardians or teachers. A good legal system will allow children to exercise more rights as they grow older. Some of these ideas are expressed in the UN Convention on the Rights of the Child.

In most cases, though, it is wrong to apply different legal standards to different groups. In some countries people from minority ethnic or religious groups have fewer rights than people from the majority group. People might lose some of their legal rights when they become prisoners, bankrupt or mentally ill. Without legal rights, people in these situations can do very little to try to help themselves.

*Under the system of apartheid in South Africa non-whites (Africans, Indians and people of mixed race) were given less rights than whites (Europeans). All public facilities were separate – those for whites were much better.*

The group that has the longest history of unequal or no legal rights is women. In nineteenth-century Britain a woman had few legal rights. If she was single she was considered to be the 'chattel' (property) of her father, and when she married, of her husband. All her property belonged to her husband. After a long campaign the situation started to change. Later, women had to fight for the right to vote, and to receive pay equal to men's for equal work. Today, although the law in Britain says women are equal to men, women do not always receive equal treatment.

Women still face legal discrimination in many countries. For example, in Pakistan and Iran, where the governments promote very strict forms of Islam, the word of a woman is considered to be worth only half of the word of a man. So even if a woman is allowed to appear in a court as a witness, she needs at least one more woman to support her evidence to make it equal to a man's.

In most countries, people who are not citizens of the country in which they live do not have the same legal rights as citizens. They may not know what legal rights they possess or how they can use them. This is what happened to Adah when she came to live in Britain. Adah tells her story:

'I was born in Ghana. My dad died when I was very young and later my mum married a Ghanaian man who was a British citizen. When he returned to Britain, my mum went with him. I stayed with my grandma in Ghana, but she died when I was ten, so I went to live in my uncle's house. After I left school I wanted to work, but there weren't any jobs. My uncle said that I was just another mouth to feed and I should leave.

*This English woman in 1914 chained herself to the railings of Buckingham Palace as part of the campaign for the right of women to vote. This right was finally won for all women in England in 1928.*

*Migrants are good for the economy, bringing skills to their new country and buying the goods and services it produces. This young African woman works as a secretary in a busy London office and attends evening courses in business studies at her local college.*

'I had often asked my mum if I could come to live with her but she said that my stepfather wasn't keen. Now my uncle kept on saying that I must go soon because once I was eighteen, I wouldn't be able to enter Britain as a dependent [as a child]. But there were so many hold-ups in getting a passport and an air ticket that I didn't leave Ghana until a week after my eighteenth birthday.

'Luckily, in those days Ghanaians didn't need visas to enter Britain. The immigration officer said that I could stay for six months although I wasn't allowed to work, and that I could apply for an extension to my visa later. I was overjoyed to be with my mother again. But I soon realized that my stepfather was a violent man and my mother lived in constant fear of him. He took my passport and said he'd keep it safe for me. I didn't see it again for three years.

'I wanted to be independent and I soon found a place on a training scheme in office skills. I studied hard and was overjoyed when I graduated top of the class. But my six-month visa was running out and I wanted to extend it. My stepfather said he would do it for me and get me a work permit. I didn't really trust him but he frightened me.

*A housing advice centre in England. Advice centres help people who have problems with the government authorities.*

'I searched for an office job and finally found one in a small publishing company. I did typing and reception work and my company seemed pleased with me. I finally plucked up the courage to leave home. I tried to get my passport from my stepfather but he refused to give it to me.

'One day the police arrived at the office. They said that I was an illegal immigrant. They asked for my passport but of course I didn't have it. They said that I should go to the police station, but my colleagues persuaded the police that they would guarantee my attendance when the police needed me. They helped me to find an immigration lawyer at a legal advice centre.

'The lawyer had to get a court order to make my stepfather hand back my passport. Then she wrote a long letter of appeal to the British Home Office, explaining that, although technically I was in Britain illegally, I had lived here for over three years, I was financially independent, and I had no real family in Ghana and no job prospects there.

The letter pointed out how my stepfather had taken my passport and lied about my visa. It asked that the Home Office allow me to stay in Britain.

'It took the Home Office a year to reply. They rejected my application and said I should be deported to Ghana within two weeks. I was devastated. The legal advice centre registered an appeal on my behalf and the deportation was postponed until the appeal could be heard. We contacted my Member of Parliament (MP) who agreed to approach the Home Office.

'Finally, the Home Office changed its mind. I was given permission to stay for another year, and to apply for permanent residence after that. However, I wasn't allowed to work, so I had to leave my job at the publishing company. At the end of the year I made another application to stay and this time it was accepted.

'It was a hard fight and I had to learn a lot about legal matters. I was lucky because I had good friends who knew how the system worked and how to find free legal help. If I'd had to pay lawyers it would have been very expensive. But at times I felt that because I was a foreigner I had hardly any human rights.'

*Refugees, who are forced to flee their own country because they fear for their safety, face particular difficulties when they arrive in a new country. They need to learn a new language and way of life. These Vietnamese refugees are staying in a reception centre before moving to permanent housing.*

# 5

# Punishment and the death penalty

IT is generally accepted that if a person is found guilty of committing a crime, he or she should be punished. But what is the reason for this? Is it to make people pay for their crimes, to stop others from committing similar crimes, or to re-educate offenders and give them a new chance in life, so that they do not continue to commit crimes in the future? These three elements can be called punishment, deterrence and rehabilitation.

When a person is tried and found guilty it is the duty of the court to decide on the sentence. There are several basic principles that govern the type and length of sentence. One is equity. It would be wrong to give two people who committed the same crime under the same circumstances very different sentences. Thus judges are given guidelines to assist them. Even so, in many countries there are wide variations in sentencing.

*A young offender being taken into custody in a police station in Britain. (Posed by model.)*

Another principle is that a sentence should not be more severe than the crime. For example, a person who commits a relatively minor crime should not receive a severe sentence. Similarly, a first-time offender should not receive the same sentence as someone who has been convicted previously. When a sentence is very severe, then the elements of punishment and deterrence are much greater than that of rehabilitation.

A third principle is that a sentence should not be cruel or inhuman. The United Nations' *Standard Minimum Rules for the Treatment of Prisoners* gives detailed rules to ensure that the basic human rights of all prisoners are respected. It says that prisoners are entitled to reasonable standards of food, accommodation and cleanliness, should have access to visitors, exercise and medical services, and should not be subject to unnecessary or violent punishment.

*Instead of going to prison, this Hispanic (Spanish-speaking) boy is doing community service painting houses in a poor neighbourhood of Texas, USA.*

But the ideas of what is a fair, reasonable and humane sentence have varied from place to place and era to era. For example, in France before the revolution of 1789, if a poor person was suspected of the theft of a lace handkerchief or a piece of meat, it was common to whip him or her brutally or to have the person imprisoned without trial.

Today, a person who had committed a similar crime might be cautioned, fined or told to do community service. Thus, a teenager who had stolen money from an old people's home might be sentenced to community service there, both as a punishment for the crime and as a chance for rehabilitation. Hopefully, the experience would also act as a deterrent to further crimes. But today in some countries a teenager committing a similar crime would be almost as harshly sentenced as in eighteenth-century France.

The ultimate sentence is the death penalty. Some people feel that when a murder takes place the only appropriate punishment is to kill the murderer. In support of their opinion they might repeat the biblical saying 'an eye for an eye...' However, in some countries the death penalty is used for lesser crimes than murder, such as robbery or drug abuse, or against political prisoners. Those countries that retain the death penalty claim that it acts as a deterrent against others committing similar crimes, although in fact there is good evidence to the contrary.

Campaigners against the death penalty point out that the punishment cannot be reversed – after execution there is no possibility of appeal or rehabilitation. Sometimes innocent people are executed. Any method of execution – such as hanging, shooting, electrocution or lethal injection – will always be cruel and painful. They claim that by using the death penalty, society itself is acting as a murderer.

About half of the world's countries, including most Western countries, no longer follow a policy of executing those found guilty of serious crimes. But other countries retain and use the death penalty. Some use it rarely, but others use it frequently. In China and Nigeria the death sentence is carried out quickly and publicly and the prisoners have little or no chance to appeal against it.

But while the death penalty has been abolished in most Western countries, it has been used ever more frequently in the USA. In 1992, 36 of the 51 state governments kept the death penalty as the ultimate punishment and about a dozen states used it to execute prisoners. Most of these states are in the south of the USA and they include Texas, Louisiana, Alabama and Florida.

In 1972 the US Supreme Court ruled that all existing state death penalty laws were invalid, saying that the way that they were applied amounted to 'cruel and unusual punishment'. However, it didn't ban the death penalty and 36 states introduced new legislation allowing it. For ten years, from 1966 until 1976, no executions were carried out anywhere in the USA. Hundreds of prisoners who had been sentenced under the old laws waited for years on 'death row'.

Then, in 1977, states began to apply their new death penalty laws, at first slowly and then in increasing numbers. From 1977 to 1982, six prisoners were executed. In 1987, twenty-five prisoners were executed. In 1992 there were thirty-one executions. More people were being sentenced to death. In 1982 there were 1,100 prisoners on death row, in 1987 there were almost 2,000 and in 1992 there were 2,600.

One of the prisoners who spent thirteen years on death row in the state of Louisiana before he was executed in 1990, was Dalton Prejean. Like many of the death row prisoners, Dalton was a black American. Although all Americans are equal under the law, black Americans, Native Americans and other ethnic minorities often face discrimination. Furthermore, according to US government statistics, 33 per cent of black Americans live in poverty, and, as we saw in chapter 3, it is very difficult to obtain justice if you are poor. Statistics show that black Americans are much more likely to be convicted and sentenced to death than whites who have committed similar crimes.

*One of the ways of carrying out the death penalty in the USA is by using the electric chair. The prisoner is strapped into the chair and powerful bolts of electricity are passed through his or her body.*

*Dalton Prejean, who spent thirteen years on death row before he was executed.*

Dalton's story shows the injustice of the death penalty. As a child Dalton had suffered years of mental cruelty and physical abuse from his guardians and this had resulted in brain damage and some learning difficulties. Dalton never had a chance to live the normal life of a child and it wasn't surprising that he grew into a violent teenager. Dalton was only seventeen years old when he was sentenced to death, after being convicted of killing a policeman. But the jury that convicted him was not told of his background or his particular problems by either Dalton's lawyer or by the judge. At least one member of the jury later said that he would have considered the case differently had he known the full facts.

Prisoners condemned to death in the USA are not immediately executed. There are many ways in which prisoners and their lawyers can try to reverse the sentence. Some prisoners may be innocent of the crime for which they were convicted, others may have suffered an unfair trial, in other cases there might be mitigating circumstances – circumstances which mean that the prisoner was not fully responsible for his or her actions. One mitigating circumstance is the age of the prisoner.

International law says that children (i.e., people under eighteen) need special protection and should certainly not be treated like adult prisoners or be executed. International law also says that people who have learning difficulties or who suffer from mental illness should not be executed. But in 1989 the US Supreme Court ruled that it was 'constitutional' to execute juvenile offenders and people with learning difficulties.

*The cells on death row in a Louisiana prison.*

Dalton Prejean's lawyers tried many times to overturn his death sentence. They admitted his guilt but pointed out his youth at the time of the killing and his mental problems. But the appeals were rejected even though the Pardons and Parole Board of Louisiana recommended that his sentence be reduced to life imprisonment.

Death row is a lonely and frightening place. Dalton was kept in a tiny cell, without an outside view, and let out only for exercise and occasional visits from his lawyers and family. Many inmates of death row have said that the endless waiting and uncertainty are as bad as the death sentence itself. But the appeals process is their only hope.

Dalton Prejean was executed by electrocution in 1990. The state claims that this is a quick and painless method of execution. However, some prisoners do not lose consciousness and die instantly, but linger in agony for several minutes. Shortly before he died Dalton said: 'I don't ask to get out of prison. I just ask to live with my mistake . . . I've changed. There's a whole difference between being seventeen and being thirty.'

# 6

# Justice denied by the State: 'disappearances' and illegal killings

A 'DISAPPEARANCE' is when a person or persons are taken by a country's police, army or other government force and are kept in secret detention. Often, after denying any such incident, the government claims it has no knowledge of the 'disappeared'. Usually, the security forces come unexpectedly at night and drag the person from their home, but sometimes they take people off the street in front of witnesses.

In most cases, the 'disappeared' are never seen alive again. They may be killed soon after their detention, or they may be kept in prison and tortured for many years before finally being killed. Often, many years later, their remains are found in unmarked graves; very occasionally, they are released from detention, as happened in Morocco in 1991 when many people who were 'disappeared' in 1973 were finally released.

Illegal killing is the outright murder of a country's citizens by agents of the government, or by private armies whose crimes are ignored or approved by the government. It may involve individuals, or it may be the mass murder of whole villages of people or sections of the population.

> **And Now She's Losing Her First Teeth**
>
> and that one there who's that
> next to Uncle Roberto?
>   why little one, that's your father.
> why doesn't my daddy come home?
>   because he can't.
> is daddy dead
> since he never comes home?
>   and if I tell her that her daddy
>   is alive
>   I am lying
>   and if I tell her that her daddy
>   is dead
>   I am lying.
> So I tell her the only thing I can tell her which is not a lie:
>   he doesn't come home because he can't.
>
> *by Ariel Dorfman, Chilean exile, about the 'disappeared'*

*A woman holding a photograph of one of the 'disappeared' at a demonstration by GAM, a Guatemalan human rights organization, in Guatemala City.*

When the government acts like the worst kind of criminal towards its own people, this is a total denial of the right to justice for the individual. Why does it happen? 'Disappearances' and illegal killings are most often used by dictatorships or by military governments which have taken power by force, not by the democratic process. Sometimes, governments that claim to be democratic, such as the Indian Government, also commit such crimes.

Governments that do not have the support of their people use these violent methods to control them, to frighten them into accepting an illegal system of rule. In this way, opposition groups trying to restore democracy and working for improvements in people's lives can be wiped out. Trade unionists, teachers, students, community workers, nuns, priests and ordinary men and women all over the world have suffered like this.

Illegal killings are also used by governments to get rid of people they consider to be undesirable, such as members of certain ethnic minorities, or petty criminals. In urban areas of Colombia, South America, government 'death squads' have killed scores of suspected lawbreakers; in Iraq, hundreds of Kurds and many Assyrian Christians have been 'disappeared'.

*In the film* Missing, *set in Chile, an American woman searches for her journalist partner who has been 'disappeared' by the military authorities.*

'Disappearances' took place in twenty countries and illegal killings in forty-five countries in 1991, according to Amnesty International. But the use of 'disappearances' as a political weapon is usually associated with countries in Latin America. After the military coup in Chile in 1973, about 1,000 people were known to have 'disappeared' after being arrested by the new Pinochet government. In Argentina in 1976, a military coup began years of terror during which it is estimated that the 'disappearances' ran into thousands.

Despite the abuse of power by the government and the atmosphere of suspicion and fear, many people in Argentina refused to be silenced. What can people do when their right to justice is ignored? One means is to go to the police station and ask for a writ of *Habeas Corpus*; this is a Latin phrase meaning 'you must have the body'. The person named must be brought before a judge and either charged or released. This is what many people tried to do in Argentina. But the government refused to operate this process and when thousands are missing, *Habeas Corpus* cannot work.

Of the thousands in Argentina who were 'disappeared', large numbers were young people of both sexes, whose mothers began a frantic search for them. One mother describes her experiences: 'My son was only fourteen when he was "disappeared". He was taken from his school by men in plain clothes. Other children and some teachers saw what happened and the head teacher immediately rang the local police station. They told him that the army had my son and that he would be released after questioning. The head teacher came to tell me and told me to wait until the next day. He was sure everything would be alright.

'My son was a good boy, there was no reason why the police should have taken him, even in those bad times. It didn't make any sense. We waited until the next day, but there was no sign of him. I decided to go to the police station and demand to see the Chief of Police. My husband said it was dangerous, that they might take me too. But I could not stop crying, I had to do something to find my son.

*The Mothers of the 'Disappeared' in Argentina gathering in 1984 to mark International Women's Day. On March 8 women world-wide celebrate their work for women's rights.*

'In the months that followed, I went to every police station, army barracks, detention centre and prison in the district to beg for my son. The local police station now told me the head teacher had lied, they said that they had never heard of my son. Everywhere I went, I heard nothing but denials. It felt like a nightmare. My family were in a daze, we could not give up hope, but we felt so helpless.

'I started to meet other women at police stations, other women who had lost their children. We all felt the same, what could we do? Who would listen? One day someone said we must make the world listen, we must hold a demonstration to ask where our children were. If we all stood together they could not 'disappear' all of us.

'So one day in April 1977, we all went to the main square in the capital, Buenos Aires. The word had spread and there were many women, mothers and grandmothers, and we had all brought photos of our children, and banners. We did not speak, we marched in silence. We have marched every week for over fifteen years now, long since the military *junta* was overthrown in 1983.

'Some women got their children back alive; others found a body in a morgue. I have never seen my son again. People ask us why we still march. We march for the truth, for someone to take responsibility for these crimes. We must have justice, for our lost children and for ourselves.'

---

*Anniversary*

And every 19th September
– it will be four years
how could so much time have gone by –
I will have to ask her again
if there is any news,
if something has been learned.

and she, no, no thank you,
I appreciate your kindness,
while her eyes continue saying
what they said to me without words
that first time
– it will be three years now,
how can it be –
that no, no thank you,
I appreciate the kindness,
but I am not a widow,
and don't come any closer,
and don't suggest a thing,
and I will not marry you,
and I am not a widow,
yet.

*Ariel Dorfman*

# 7
# Justice in our lives

ROSA and Iqbal are two ordinary fourteen-year-old pupils at a school in Vancouver, Canada. They are lucky, they live in a lovely part of the country and they go to a school with many facilities. The school runs lots of clubs and activities at lunchtime, after school and at weekends. Most of the activities are supervised by teachers, but Rosa and Iqbal also organize activities in their free time, working with their school friends.

*This young woman in Vancouver, Canada, is painting a child's face as part of a big festival. All the money raised at the festival goes to charity.*

These two young people are the representatives for their year on the school's Charity Committee. That might sound very serious, but the idea of the Committee is for pupils to learn about the work of different charities, to raise money for them and have fun while they are doing it.

The Committee has two representatives from each year group in the school, who hold office for an academic year. The Committee decides which organizations it will focus on each term and tries to collect as much information as possible about the work that they do. Then they invite someone from each charity to come to the school and talk to the pupils. During this visit the Committee presents the visitor with money which the pupils have collected.

So what has all that got to do with the right to justice? Whatever our age, we are all part of a society. Within that society, we are part of a community and we have a role to play in it. It is like being a piece in a jigsaw puzzle; we all have a special place.

*The Indian girls in this picture are painting on the subject of human rights for an Amnesty International competition.*

*Mayan men in Guatemala wearing traditional clothes. The Maya are the original people of Guatemala, but they suffer terrible discrimination. They own the poorest land and many live in poverty. In the 1960s the Maya began to campaign for fair treatment.*

When you are a young teenager you might belong to several communities, but all young people belong to at least two – the family (whatever form that takes) and school. You might also belong to some kind of club, a music group or a religious community.

Rosa and Iqbal, as part of their school community, chose to work with others in their school and take an interest in the world outside their small town. By doing this, they have found out about what is happening to the environment; about poverty, not only in Africa, but in many parts of their own country; and about children who live in places where their human rights are not respected.

At another school, in London, England, the school librarian told some pupils about the Maya, the indigenous peoples of Guatemala, who are struggling for their rights. The pupils wanted to do something to show those people that they knew about their suffering and they cared about them, so they sent Christmas cards to a human rights group in Guatemala.

Over the next six years the pupils' interest developed into a whole range of activities. At school, they held assemblies and concerts on the subject, worked on projects about Guatemala for their exams, wrote letters to children there and put together two exhibitions – one about the situation in Guatemala and another about their support work. They also compiled a magazine to sell to other schools to raise money, entertained visitors from Guatemala, and spoke to their MPs about the situation there. In 1991 they were sent a huge banner made by Guatemalan children to thank them for their care and support. They have now made their own banner to send back to those children.

These schoolchildren in Canada and England have made links with people in the rest of the world. They have shown that they are global citizens, members of the biggest community that exists. We have seen how even the youngest children can understand the idea of fairness. What all these young people are doing is showing not only that they understand what human rights are, but that they also want to work with those people whose rights are being denied.

*The banner received by pupils in London from Guatemala. It reads: 'Children of GAM, still we ask, still we dream, still we hope.'*

According to the law in most European countries, young people have the right to education until they are at least sixteen. That is part of the right to social justice. Some countries only make education available until the age of eleven, the minimum stated in the Universal Declaration of Human Rights. But with rights come responsibilities and duties. Those responsibilities and duties might be found in rules or laws which must be followed. Alternatively, they might be moral responsibilities which are sometimes more difficult to understand.

*In 'Operation a Day's Work' in 1989, Norwegian pupils took a job for a day and gave their pay to charity.*

Rights can never be separated from responsibilities and duties. Those people who want to claim their rights without performing their duties will come into conflict with the law and with other people in their community. This all sounds complicated, but most of the time we claim our rights or have them given to us and we understand our responsibilities and perform our duties without even thinking about it.

*Adopted children from many backgrounds can live together as a family and learn to take responsibility for one another.*

Parents and guardians have a legal responsibility to make sure that their children go to school. Most people know how important a good education is for their children, but there are some people who keep their children away from schools simply because of how much they care about this education. They may be concerned that the school is not providing the kind of education that reflects their own beliefs and values. Parents may say that their religious faith is not catered for at the school or that the school is not strict enough with the children. This is where conflicts can arise between the right of the child to an education, the parents' right to a school of their choice, and the legal and moral responsibility of the state to educate the child. Sometimes there are moral problems with rights that are not easy to solve.

You may think that because you are under eighteen, you have no legal rights and therefore, no responsibilities and duties. This is not actually true. In Britain, for example, children have legal rights from birth, which increase as they get older until at eighteen they are legally independent and become citizens with the right to vote.

From birth they have the right to open a bank account and by twelve they can go and buy a pet on their own. Just think how many responsibilities are involved with owning a pet!

On top of legal responsibilities, there are also moral duties. Relationships with the people we live with bring rights and responsibilities from an early age, which change as we get older and the people and the relationships alter. At any age we all have moral responsibilities towards parents and guardians. If you have younger brothers and sisters, or live with younger children, you will have more rights than they have. You may be allowed to stay out later perhaps, but you may also have to take on the responsibility of looking after them on some occasions.

At school you obey rules that exist to make life safe and orderly. Not running in the corridor may be frustrating when you are in a hurry, but it makes sense; if all the pupils were running about, someone might get hurt.

*Looking after a pet involves a number of responsibilities.*

In this case you are being expected to act responsibly and think about everyone's safety, not just your own convenience. These may all seem like unimportant examples, but they help us to understand about duties and responsibilities. As we grow older, so our responsibilities grow. When we reach eighteen, legally we become 'adult', and we gain rights that carry with them much larger duties and responsibilities.

In other parts of this book we have seen how many people's rights are taken away altogether, how some people's rights are inferior to those of others, and where certain barriers may stop people from claiming their rights.

The abuse of people's right to justice can vary enormously, from being denied the right to live, to losing the right to belong to a trade union. But who should be protecting everyone's right to justice, whether it be legal, social or economic?

In some instances people help themselves and find ways to use the rights that they still have to regain those they have lost. The 'Mothers of the Disappeared' in Argentina are a good example of this. Others try to persuade people who are more powerful than themselves, such as politicians and lawyers, to fight for people's rights. But many people shrug their shoulders and say, 'What can I do?' Then there

*Rigoberta Menchu, a Mayan leader from Guatemala, at a demonstration for Mayan rights. In 1992 she won the Nobel Peace Prize.*

> THE GENERAL ASSEMBLY
>
> *proclaims*
>
> THIS UNIVERSAL DECLARATION OF HUMAN RIGHTS as a common standard of achievement for all peoples and all nations, to the end that every individual and every organ of society, keeping this Declaration constantly in mind, shall strive by teaching and education to promote respect for these rights and freedoms and by progressive measures, national and international, to secure their universal and effective recognition and observance, both among the peoples of Member States themselves and among the peoples of territories under their jurisdiction.
>
> **Article 1.** All human beings are born free and equal in dignity and rights. They are endowed with reason and conscience and should act towards one another in a spirit of brotherhood.
>
> **Article 2.** Everyone is entitled to all the rights and freedoms set forth in this Declaration, without distinction of any kind, such as race, colour, sex, language, religion, political or other opinion, national or social origin, property, birth or other status.
>
> Furthermore, no distinction shall be made on the basis of the political, jurisdictional or international status of the country or territory to which a person belongs, whether it be independent, trust, non-self-governing or under any other limitation of sovereignty.
>
> **Article 3.** Everyone has the right to life, liberty and security of person.
>
> **Article 4.** No one shall be held in slavery or servitude; slavery and the slave trade shall be prohibited in all their forms.
>
> **Article 5.** No one shall be subjected to torture or to cruel, inhuman or degrading treatment or punishment.
>
> **Article 6.** Everyone has the right to recognition everywhere as a person before the law.

*This is the first part of the Universal Declaration of Human Rights, which was adopted in 1948.*

are others, like the street children of Guatemala or the very poor in India, who, for many years, had no idea that they had any rights as human beings, until community workers set up special education programmes for them.

As the United Nations has written: 'People must first know what their rights are in order to be able to enjoy them ... We have repeatedly emphasized the importance of information and education on human rights at all levels of society.' That is why the introduction to the Universal Declaration of Human Rights contains a very important message, which is that all countries in the United Nations must make sure that the Declaration is displayed and taught in schools and colleges everywhere. After all, what good are rights that come from natural justice if you have no knowledge of them and no way of claiming them?

The message from the UN may have been lost over the years, but what is happening every time a school holds a sponsored bike ride and gives that money to a human rights organization; every time a student writes to a local paper about the position of the homeless; every time a youth club holds a Christmas dinner for an old people's home? In a small way they are all joining in the protection and promotion of the right to justice for themselves, for the street child and for the 'disappeared' all over the world.

# Glossary

**Amnesty International** An organization that works world-wide for the release of prisoners of conscience, fair trials for political prisoners and an end to torture, executions without trial, 'disappearances' and the death penalty.

**Appeal** A request to a higher court to change the judgement given by a lower court, based on new or misunderstood evidence.

**Arrest warrant** The document that gives the reasons for an arrest.

**Bail** Money pledged (usually by family or friends) to the court in order to gain the temporary release of a charged person, and to ensure that he or she will be available for trial when needed.

**Caution** An official warning.

**Charge** The reason given for an arrest.

**Citizenship** Membership of a state, involving rights, responsibilities and duties.

**Community service** Voluntary unpaid work for the general good, often given as an alternative to jail for first-time offenders or for less serious crimes.

**Constitution** The basic rules and customs that state how a country is to be organized and governed.

**Coup** (full form: *coup d'état*) A violent or illegal takeover of government.

**Court order** A document issued by a court.

**Cross-examination** Questioning by both the prosecution and defence in court.

**Custody** Temporary imprisonment.

**Defence** The lawyer and others who act for an arrested person in court.

**Democracy** Rule by a government that is elected by the people.

**Detention** Imprisonment.

**Detention centre** A place of imprisonment.

**Deterrence** The stopping or preventing of something.

**Dictatorship** Government by a person or people who have not been elected and are not responsible to any legal or moral system.

**Entitlement** A right to do or to have something.

**Equity** Equality or sameness.

**Ethnic minority** A group of people who share a language, religion, culture or way of life which makes them feel different to the majority population.

**Evidence** An account of the facts of a case, given in court.

**First-time offender** A person who is found guilty of a crime for the first time.

**Gender** The state of being male or female.

**Guardian** A person who takes legal responsibility for a child who is not his or her own.

**Home Office** The government department in Britain that is mainly responsible for public order and immigration.

**Humane** Treating people in a way that respects their human rights.

**Humanitarian** Showing sympathy and kindness towards other people.

*Junta* A group of military officers which runs the government of a country, usually after a coup.

**Labour camp** A very harsh prison where prisoners have to do hard work.

**Legal advice centre** A place where a person can get free advice on legal matters.

**Mental illness** A condition in which a person's mind and emotions are so deeply upset that he or she cannot cope with most aspects of ordinary life.

**Moral** Concerned with right and wrong behaviour and duty to others.

**Political prisoner** A person who is in detention because the government says that his or her political beliefs or actions are harmful.

**Prosecution** The authority (usually the government or police) that takes legal action against a person or an organization in court.

**Rehabilitation** The helping of a person to readapt to society after a mental illness or time in prison.

**Security forces** The collective name for the military and police forces.

**Serfs** People who, in medieval Europe, were not free, but were thought of as belonging to the lord who owned the land they lived on.

**Sexual orientation** A person's preference for a certain kind of sexual activity, i.e., heterosexual, homosexual, bisexual or celibate.

**Torture** Severe physical or mental ill-treatment.

**Trial** An examination in a law court by a judge and jury to decide an issue, usually the guilt or innocence of a person.

**Visa** An entry in a person's passport that gives permission to visit another country.

**Work permit** A document that allows a person (usually a foreigner) the right to work in a country.

# Further reading

Recommended age range appears after each entry.

*A Bill of Rights*: Liberty Briefing No. 13, (National Council for Civil Liberties, 1989) European Convention on Human Rights as a basis for a new British Bill of Rights. 16–18

*Black People, White Justice? Race and the Criminal Justice System* by A Shallice and P Gordon (Runnymede Trust, 1990) Black people and their treatment by the courts in Britain. 16–18

*The Case Against Capital Punishment* (Howard League, 1987)

*Do it Justice: Resources and Activities for Introducing Education in Human Rights* (Birmingham Development Education Centre, 1988) Primary and early secondary.

*Education Rights Handbook* (Children's Legal Centre, 1987) Rules and punishments in school, welfare, health, etc. 16–18

*Freedom, the Individual and the Law* by Geoffrey Robertson (Penguin, 1989) 16–18

Gay Research Reports: *1. Something to Tell You*; *2. Talking About School*; *3. Talking About Young Lesbians*; *4. Talking About Youth Work* by Lorraine Trenchard and Hugh Warren (Lesbian and Gay Teenage Groups, 1987) 15–18

*A Guide to Parliament* (Children's Legal Centre, 1988) Information sheet on the processes in the British Parliament. 11–15

*Human Rights* by Jane Sherwin (Wayland, 1989) Introduction to the human rights tragedies of the past century. 11–15

*Let's Discuss Women's Rights* by Barbara Einhorn (Wayland, 1988) Case studies in areas of rights, health, work and violence. 11–15

*The Long Arm of the Law* by Gwyneth Vorhaus (Wayland, 1986) Outlines legal, court and police procedures. 11–15

*Minority Rights: Do the Right Thing* by Rachel Warner (Minority Rights Group, 1992) Practical guide to what minority rights are and how young people can support them. 11–18

*New Rights for Children* (Save the Children Fund/UNICEF, 1990) A response to the Convention of the Rights of the Child. 9–14

*Rights: Thinking about Moral and Social Issues* by Derek Wright (Pergamon Educational, 1987) Takes a close look at the UN Declaration of Human Rights. 11–15

*Roots of Racism* (Institute of Race Relations, 1986) Four parts: *Roots of Racism*; *Patterns of Racism*; *How Racism Came to Britain*; *The Fight Against Racism*. 11–15

*Understanding the Law* (Edward Arnold, 1988) Four-part teaching pack: *The Individual and Society*; *Implementing the Law*; *Using the Law*; *Going to Work*. 16-18

*Unequal Justice* by Robert Perske (Abingdon Press, Nashville, 1991) About Americans with learning difficulties encountering the criminal justice system.

*Why Human Rights?* (Amnesty International, 1987) Video-based pack with worksheets focusing on Amnesty's specific human rights concerns. 14–18

*Working for Freedom: A Human Rights Education Pack* (Amnesty International, 1991) Classroom resource to show teachers how human rights can be taught throughout the curriculum. 11–18

*Young People's Rights* by Marion Wright (Optima, 1990) Practical guide for dealing with the law. 11–15

# Useful addresses

**Australia**

Amnesty International
Australian Section
Private Bag 23, Broadway
Sydney, NSW, 2007

Human Rights and Equal
Opportunities Commission
PO Box 5218
Sydney, NSW, 2001

**Britain**

Amnesty International British
Section
99-119 Roseberry Ave
London EC1R 4RE
(071 814 6200)

Anti-Slavery International
180 Brixton Rd
London SW9 6AT
(071 582 4040)

Centre for World
Development Education
(CWDE)
1 Catton St
London WC1R 4AB
(071 831 3844)

Children's Legal Centre
20 Compton Terrace
London N1 2UN
(071 359 6251)

The Citizenship Foundation
63 Charterhouse St
London EC1M 6HJ
(071 253 4480)

Commission for Racial
Equality
Elliot House
10–12 Allington St
London SW1E 5EH
(071 828 7022)

Council of Europe
Publications from
HMSO Agency Section
51 Nine Elms Lane
London SW8 5RD

The Howard League for
Penal Reform
708 Holloway Rd
London N19 3NL
(071 281 7722)

Institute of Education
Curriculum Resources
Library
20 Bedford Way
London WC1H 0AL
(071 580 1122)

Minority Rights Group
379 Brixton Rd
London SW9 7DE
(071 978 9498)

Oxfam Youth and Education
Department
274 Banbury Rd
Oxford, OX2 7DZ
(0865 312353)

United Nations Association
3 Whitehall Court
London SW1A 2EL
(071 930 2931)

Women's International
Resource Centre
173 Archway Rd
London N6 5BL
(081 341 4403)

**Canada**

Amnesty International
Canadian Section (English-speaking)
130 Slater St, Suite 900
Ottawa, Ontario, K1P 6E2

Amnistie Internationale
Section Canadienne (French-speaking)
6250 Boulevard Monk
Montreal, Quebec, H4E 3H7

Canadian Human Rights
Commission
Place de Ville Tower A
320 Queen St, 13th Floor
Ottawa, Ontario, K1A 1E1

**Ireland**

Amnesty International
Irish Section
Sean McBride House
8 Shaw St
Dublin 2

**New Zealand**

Amnesty International
New Zealand Section
PO Box 793
Wellington

Human Rights Commission
PO Box 5054
Lambton Quay
Wellington

**USA**

Amnesty International of the
USA (AIUSA)
322 Eighth Avenue
New York, NY, 10001

Human Rights Watch
485 Fifth Ave,
New York, NY, 10017

Lawyers Committee for
Human Rights
330 Seventh Ave
New York, NY, 10001

# Index

Entries in **bold** indicate subjects shown in pictures as well as in the text.

Americans, black 27, **28**
Argentina 32-4, 42

Britain 8, 20-23, 37, 40
   immigration into 20-23

Canada 7, **35**
charity work 36-8, **39**
children's rights 9, 19, 28-9, 38, 39, 40, 41, 43
Chile 32
China 8, 11-14, 26
community service **25**
constitutional law 10
constitution 7, 8
   Indian 16
   US 28
Convention on the Rights of the Child 9
crime 24-8

death in police custody 18
death penalty 26-9
death row **29**
democracy 8, 13
'disappearances' 30-34

education 7, 9, 12-13, 15-16, 37-8, 39, 40

GAM (Guatemalan human rights organization) 31, 38
Ghanaians 20-23
Guatemala 31, 37-8, 43

*habeas corpus* 32
Home Office, British 22, 23
Hood, Robin **5**

illegal killings 18, 30-31
immigration (into Britain) 20-23
India 15-18, 31, 36, 43
   caste system 16, 18
   constitution 16

justice
   economic 7, 9, 16
   legal 9, 10-14
   natural 4-5, 8
   for poor people 15-18
   social 6-7, 9, 16, 39

law 7, 8
   Chinese 11-14
   constitutional 10
   criminal 10-11
   international 8, 9, 28
legal rights 15, 19, 20, 22-3
legal systems
   British 22-3
   Chinese 11-14
   Indian 16-18
   US 26-7, 28, 29

Maya 37-8
Menchu, Rigoberta **42**
Mothers of the 'Disappeared' **33**

Prejean, Dalton 27-9
prisoners, treatment of 25
   in Argentina 33-4
   in China **13**, 14
   in India 17-18
   in the USA 28-9
punishment 6, 24-6

refugees **23**
rights and responsibilities 6, 9, 13, 39, 40-42

South Africa **19**
Student Councils 7

Tiananmen Square **12**, 13
Tubman, Harriet 7

United Nations 8, **9**, 25, 43
Universal Declaration of Human Rights **8,** 9, **39**, **43**
US Supreme Court 27, 28
USA 8, 14, 25, 26-8

women's rights 20, 33, 34
   legal discrimination against 20

Zedong, Mao **11**